AF538367

ל

Lamed

לִימוֹנָדָה

Limonadah

Lemonade

מ

Mem

מָגֵן דָוִד

Magayn David

Star of David

נ

Nun

נֶגֶב

Negev

Negev

Samech

סַנְדָלִים

Sandalim

Sandals

Ayin

עִבְרִית

Ivrit

Hebrew

פ

Pey

פָלָאפֶל

Falafel

Falafel

צ

Tsade

צְפָת

Ts'fat

Tsfat

Kof

קִיבּוּץ

Kibbutz

Kibbutz

Resh

רִיקוּדֵי עַם

Rikuday Am

Folk Dancing

Shin

שׁוּק

Shuk

Market

Tav

תֵּל אָבִיב

Tayl Aviv

Tel Aviv

Aleph

אֶרֶץ יִשְׂרָאֵל

Eretz Yisra-ayl

The Land of Israel

Bet

בֵּית כְּנֶסֶת

Bayt K'neset

Synagogue

Gimmel

גֶּפֶן

Gefen

Vine

Dalet

דֶּגֶל יִשְׂרָאֵל

Degel Yisra-ayl

Israeli Flag

Hey

הַר הַחֶרְמוֹן

Har Hachermon

Mount Hermon

Vav

וַיִּצְמַן

Vaitzman

Weitzman

Zayin

זֵיתִים

Zaytim

Olives

Chet

חוֹף הַיָּם

Chof Hayam

The Beach

Tet

טְבֶרְיָה

T'vayr-yah

Tiberius

Yod

יְרוּשָׁלַיִם

Y'rushalayim

Jerusalem

Kaf

כִּנֶּרֶת

Kineret

Sea of Galilee

ת
תֵּל אָבִיב
Tel Aviv

ש
שׁוּק
Market

ר
רִיקוּדֵי עַם
Folk Dancing

ק
קִיבּוּץ
Kibbutz

צ
צְפָת
Tsfat

פ
פָלָאפֶל
Falafel

ע
עִבְרִית
Hebrew
אֲנִי קוֹרֵא

ס
סַנְדָּלִים
Sandals

נ
נֶגֶב
Negev

מ
מָגֵן דָּוִד
Star of David

ל
לְימוֹנָדָה
Lemonade

כ
כִּנֶּרֶת
Sea of Galilee

י
יְרוּשָׁלַיִם
Jerusalem

ט
טְבֵרְיָה
Tiberius

ח
חוֹף הַיָּם
The Beach

ז
זֵיתִים
Olives

ו
וַיְצְמַן
Weitzman
הנשיא הראשון
של
מדינת ישראל.
ISRAEL'S FIRST
PRESIDENT.

ה
הַר הַחֶרְמוֹן
Mount Hermon

ד
דֶגֶל יִשְׂרָאֵל
Israeli Flag

ג
גֶּפֶן
Vine

ב
בֵּית כְּנֶסֶת
Synagogue

א
אֶרֶץ יִשְׂרָאֵל
The Land of Israel

למשפחתי האהובה,
פיטר, בן יאיר, ומיקה

To my beloved family,

Peter, Ben Yair, and Mikah

Written and Illustrated by Galia Armeland

Aleph Bet Israel © 2009 by Galia Armeland

Printed in the United States.

No part of this book may be transmitted or reproduced by any means, electronic or mechanical, without written permission, except for brief quotations included in critical articles and reviews. For information, contact the publisher.

EKS Publishing Co.
PO Box 9750
Berkeley, CA 94709-0750
E-mail: orders@ekspublishing.com
Phone: (510) 251-9100
Fax: (510) 251-9102

ISBN 978-0-939144-61-7
First Printing, May 2009

Library of Congress Cataloging-in-Publication Data:
880-01 Armeland, Galia.
A [Alef] - B [Bet] Yisra'el = Aleph bet Israel / Galia Armeland.
p. cm.
ISBN 978-0-939144-61-7
1. Hebrew language--Alphabet--Juvenile literature. I. Title.
PJ4589.A75 2009
492.4'11--dc22
2009075109

Aleph Bet Israel

Written and Illustrated by Galia Armeland

EKS Publishing

Oakland, California